DATE DUE

APR 2 0 2007	

DEMCO, INC. 38-2931

Also by Yehuda Amichai

Poems

Songs of Jerusalem and Myself

Amen

Time

Love Poems

Great Tranquillity: Questions and Answers

The Selected Poetry of Yehuda Amichai

Poems of Jerusalem

Even a Fist Was Once an Open Palm with Fingers

Recent Poems by

Yehuda Amichai

Selected and translated by
Barbara and Benjamin Harshav

HarperPerennial
A Division of HarperCollins*Publishers*

FIRST EDITION

Designed by Cassandra J. Pappas

Library of Congress Cataloging-in-Publication Data

Amichai, Yehuda.
    [Poems. English. Selections]
    Even a fist was once an open palm with fingers : recent poems / by
  Yehuda Amichai ; selected and translated by Barbara and Benjamin
  Harshav. — 1st ed.
      p. cm.
    ISBN 0-06-055297-2 — ISBN 0-06-096869-9 (pbk.)
    1. Amichai, Yehuda—Translations, English. I. Harshav, Barbara. 1940– .
  II. Harshav, Benjamin, 1928– . III. Title.
    PJ5054.A65A245 1991
    892.4'16—dc20   90-55635

91 92 93 94 95 CC/MPC 10 9 8 7 6 5 4 3 2 1
91 92 93 94 95 CC/MPC 10 9 8 7 6 5 4 3 2 1 (pbk.)

Contents

ix Translators' Note

1 What Kind of a Person

3 Like the Streams in the Negev

5 Summer Evening in the Jerusalem Mountains

7 Anniversaries of War

13 Anniversaries of Love

20 Memories of Love

23 My Mother

25 From Jerusalem to the Sea and Back

30 Four Resurrections in the Valley of the Ghosts

34 I Am a Poor Prophet

36 Summer Evening at the Window with Psalms

38 Summer Rest and Words

40 Autumn Is Near and Memory of My Parents

42 Little Ruth

44 Sheepskin Coat

47 Man with Knapsack

49 My Son

51 Hymn to a Masseuse

53 The Greatest Desire of All

55 Deir Ayub, a Heap of Watermelons and the Rest
    of My Life

56 Changes, Mistakes, Loves

58 The First Rain on a Burned Car

60 Ramatayim

62 Deganya

64 Hadera

66 Beit Guvrin

68 Open Internalized

69 Surplus of Flowers in the World

70 Throw Pillows

71 Yom Kippur

73 A Man's Soul

74 Life

75 At the Seashore

77 Museum at Akhziv

79 I Want to Confuse the Bible

81 My Children

83　The Jews

86　The Land Knows

88　Temporary Poem of My Time

91　We Have Done Our Duty

93　This Is the Life of Promises

Translators' Note

This collection has been made from translations of a large part of Yehuda Amichai's latest book, *Gam ha-egrof haya pa'am yad petuḥa ve-etsba'ot* (Tel Aviv: Schoken, 1989). The cycles "Memories of Love" and "My Mother" are from *Me-adam ata ve-el adam tashuv* (Tel Aviv: Schoken, 1985). Thanks to Yehuda Amichai, Stanley Moss, and Ted Solotaroff for their insightful suggestions.

Even a Fist Was Once
an Open Palm
with Fingers

What Kind of a Person

"What kind of a person are you?" I heard them say
   to me.
I'm a person with a complex plumbing of the soul,
sophisticated instruments of feeling and a system
of controlled memory at the end of the twentieth
   century,
but with an old body from ancient times
and with a God even older than my body.

I'm a person for the surface of the earth.
Low places, caves and wells
frighten me. Mountain peaks
and tall buildings scare me.

I'm not like an inserted fork,
not a cutting knife, not a stuck spoon.
I'm not flat and sly
like a spatula creeping up from below.
At most I am a heavy and clumsy pestle
mashing good and bad together
for a little taste
and a little fragrance.

Arrows do not direct me. I conduct
my business carefully and quietly

like a long will that began to be written
at the moment I was born.

Now I stand at the side of the street
weary, leaning on a parking meter.
I can stand here for nothing, free.

I'm not a car, I'm a person,
a man-god, a god-man
whose days are numbered. Hallelujah.

Like the Streams in the Negev

I sit in a café in the afternoon hours.
My sons are grown, my daughter is dancing
    somewhere else.
I have no baby carriage, no newspaper, no God.

I saw a woman whose father was with me in the
    battles of the Negev,
I saw his eyes gaping in a time of trouble
and dread of death. Now they are in the face of his
    daughter,
quiet, beautiful eyes. The rest of her body—
from other places, her hair grew in a time of peace,
a different genetics, generations and times I didn't
    know.

I have many times, like many watches
on the walls of a clock shop, each one shows a
    different time.
My memories are scattered over the earth
like ashes of a person who willed before his death
to burn his body
and scatter his ashes over seven seas.

I sit. Voices talking around me
like fine ironwork on a banister,

beyond it I hear the street. The table before me
is built for easy access like a bay,
like a dock in a port, like God's hand, like bride and
   groom.

Sometimes suddenly tears of happiness well up in me
as an empty street suddenly fills up with cars
when the light changes at a distant intersection,
or like the streams in the Negev
that suddenly fill up with torrents of water from a
   distant rain.
Afterward, again silence, empty
Like the streams in the Negev, like the streams in the Negev.

Summer Evening in the Jerusalem Mountains

An empty can on a rock
lit by the last rays of the sun.
A child throws stones at it,
the can tumbles, the stone falls
the sun goes down. Between things that go down
and fall I seem to rise,
a new Isaac Newton canceling the laws of nature.
My penis like a pinecone
closed on many cells of seed.

I hear the children playing, wild grapes too
are descendants unto the third generation,
voices too are sons and great-grandsons
of voices lost forever in their joy.

In these mountains hope belongs to the place
like cisterns. Even those empty
still belong to the place like hope.

I open my mouth and sing into the world.
I have a mouth, the world has no mouth.

It must use mine if it wants
to sing into me. I and the world are equivalent.

I am more.

Anniversaries of War

Tel Gath

I brought my children to the mound where once I
   fought battles,
for them to understand the things I did do
and forgive me for the things I didn't do.

The distance between my striding legs and my head
grows bigger and I grow smaller.
Those days grow away from me,
these times grow away from me too,
and I'm in the middle, without them, on this mound
with my children.

A light afternoon wind blows
but only a few people move in the blowing wind,
bend down a little with the grass and the flowers.
Dandelions cover the mound,
you could say, as dandelions in multitude.

I brought my children to the mound
and we sat there "on its back and its side"
as in the poem by Shmuel Ha-Nagid in Spain,
a man of hills and a man of wars, like me,
who sang a lullaby to his soldiers before the battle.

Yet I did not talk to my heart, as he did,
but to my children. We were the resurrection of the
    mound,
fleeting like this springtime, eternal like it too.

Ruhama

In this wadi, we camped in the days of the war.
Many years have passed since, many victories,
many defeats. Many consolations I gathered in my life
and wasted, much sorrow have I collected and spilled
    out in vain,
many things I said, like the waves of the sea
in Ashkelon, to the west, always saying the same
    things.
But as long as I live my soul remembers
and my body ripens slowly in the flame of its own
    annals.

The evening sky bends down like the sound of a
    trumpet
above us, and the lips move like lips in a prayer
before there was any God in the world.

Here we lay by day, and at night we went to the
    battle.

The smell of the sand as it was, and the smell of
    eucalyptus leaves
as it was, and the smell of the wind as it was.

And I do now what every memory dog does:
I howl quietly
and piss a turf of remembrance around me,
no one may enter it.

Huleikat—the Third Poem about Dicky

In these hills, even the towers of oil wells
are a mere memory. Here Dicky fell,
four years older than me, like a father to me
in times of trouble and distress. Now I am older than
    him
by forty years and I remember him
like a young son, and I am his father, old and grieving.

And you, who remember only faces,
do not forget the hands stretched out,
the feet running lightly,
the words.

Remember: even the departure to terrible battles
passes by gardens and windows
and children playing, a dog barking.

Remind the fallen fruit
of its leaves and branches,
remind the sharp thorns
how soft and green they were in springtime,
and do not forget,
even a fist
was once an open palm and fingers.

The Shore of Ashkelon

Here, at the shore of Ashkelon, we reached the end of
    memory
like rivers reaching the sea.
The near past sinks into the far past,
and from the depths, the far overflows the near.
Peace to him that is far off and to him that is near.

Here, among broken statues and pillars,
I ask how did Samson bring down the temple
standing eyeless, saying: "Let me die with the
    Philistines."

Did he embrace the pillars as in a last love
or did he push them away with his arms,
to be alone in his death?

What Did I Learn in the Wars

What did I learn in the wars:
to march in time to swinging arms and legs
like pumps pumping an empty well.

To march in a row and be alone in the middle,
to dig into pillows, featherbeds, the body of a beloved
  woman,
and to yell "Mama," when she cannot hear,
and to yell "God," when I don't believe in Him,
and even if I did believe in Him
I wouldn't have told Him about the war
as you don't tell a child about grown-ups' horrors.

What else did I learn? I learned to reserve a path for
  retreat.
In foreign lands I rent a room in a hotel
near the airport or railroad station.
And even in wedding halls
always to watch the little door
with the "Exit" sign in red letters.

A battle too begins
like rhythmical drums for dancing and ends
with a "retreat at dawn." Forbidden love
and battle, the two of them sometimes end like this.

But above all I learned the wisdom of camouflage,
not to stand out, not to be recognized,
not to be apart from what's around me,
even not from my beloved.
Let them think I am a bush or a lamb,
a tree, a shadow of a tree,
a doubt, a shadow of a doubt,
a living hedge, a dead stone,
a house, a corner of a house.

If I were a prophet I would have dimmed the glow of
    the vision
and darkened my faith with black paper
and covered the magic with nets.

And when my time comes, I shall don the camouflage
    garb of my end:
the white of clouds and a lot of sky blue
and stars that have no end.

Anniversaries of Love

Anniversary of Love

Anniversary of love. A hymn from the forties.
Letters like banners waving in the wind
or folded in a cupboard. Bound up in our bundles.

"I live among orange groves,
Ramatayim or Givat Haim,
I live near the water tower.
I draw from it great strength and great love,
you will understand in years to come."

The stalk releases its smell when you break it,
leaves release their smell when you rub them
thinly between your fingers. So will our love be,
you will understand in years to come.

You will cross great distances,
but you were never in the distance between my eyes
and you never will be. You will understand.
You will be in places with no orange groves,
you will forget this love
as you forgot the child's voice
you once had. You will understand in years to come.

But We

Far away, the war started. But we
were at home. The future was close by,
it started just outside the window.

The future was yellow, the color of acacias,
and purple like bougainvillea, and its voices were
the voices of the two of us.

We loved in the orchard on the sand,
the orchard gave us its strength and we gave it ours.
And beyond the row of cypresses a train passed,
but we only heard it, didn't see.
And all the words we spoke between us
began with "but we."

And when we parted, when the war was over
these words too parted: the word "but"
remained there, the word "we" moved somewhere else.

Sixty Kilograms of Pure Love

Sixty kilograms of pure love, net femininity
built for splendor that built itself—
with no architects' blueprints, no beginning, no end.
Passionate, pure autogenetics:
a love cell begets a love cell.

What does the environment do to you,
what do changes do to you?
They make you beautiful on the outside, like a sunset,
and tickle you on the inside. You laugh,
I love you.

In the Migration of Peoples

And though we lived in the same corridor
in the same house, we met only as two strangers
meeting in the migration of peoples in ancient times,
by chance.

And though you are younger than me by many years
we are both of the same archaeological stratum in the
    future.

You take words from the same place as me,
but your words are different from mine.
The light in your hair, like the light
caught in an old photo.

Housekeys used to be big and heavy and separate
and very quiet. Now bundles of keys
small and flat, rattle and tinkle,
know a lot.

Now they write names on shirts,
once they were carved on stone.

I will be different,
like a tree made
into useful furniture.

And you will remain there beautiful
like rare glass vessels in a museum,
never again to be filled
with oil and milk, wine and mead.

Two Disappeared in the House

Two disappeared in the house.
The stone of the steps soothes the feet of those who
   ascend
as the stone that soothes the feet of those who
   descend,
as the stone that soothes the dead in their graves.
And the more the steps ascend
the less they are used,
the highest ones are like new—
for souls that leave no traces.
Like people living in high regions:
when they speak, their voices rise more melodious,
up to the singing of the angels.

Two disappeared in the house.
They turn on a light. They turn it off.
The staircase goes out through the roof into the space
    of night
like an unfinished building.

In the History of Our Love

In the history of our love, always one is
a nomadic tribe, the other a nation on its own soil.
When we changed places, it was all over.

Time will pass us by, as landscapes
move behind actors standing in their places
when they make a movie. Even the words
will pass by our lips, even the tears
will pass by our eyes. Time will pass
every one in his place.

And in the geography of the rest of our lives,
who will be an island and who a peninsula
will become clear to each of us in the rest of our lives
in nights of love with others.

In-Between

Where will we be when these flowers turn into fruit
in the narrow in-between, when the flower is no
    longer a flower
and the fruit is not yet fruit? And what a wonderful
    in-between did we make
for each other, between body and body. In-between
    eyes, between waking and sleep.
In-between twilight, not day, not night.

How your springtime dress became a summer banner,
and there it's waving in the first autumn wind.˙
How my voice was my voice no more
but, almost, like prophecy.

What a wonderful in-between we were, like soil
in the cracks of a wall, small, stubborn earth
for the bold moss, the thorny caper bush
whose bitter fruit
sweetened what we ate together.

These are the last days of books.
Then, the last days of words.
You will understand in years to come.

I Know a Man

I know a man
who took pictures of the landscape he saw
from the window of the room where he loved
and not of the face of the one he loved.

Memories of Love

Image

I cannot imagine
how we shall live without each other,
so we said.

And since then we live inside that image,
day after day, far from each other,
far from the house
where we said those words.

Every door closing, every window opening,
like under anesthesia, no pain.

Pains come later.

Terms and Conditions

We were like children who didn't want to
come out of the sea. The blue night came
and then the black night.

What did we bring back for the rest of our lives,
a flaming face, like the burning bush
that won't consume itself till the end of our lives.

We made a strange arrangement between us:
if you come to me, I'll come to you,
strange terms and conditions: if you forget me,
I'll forget you.
Strange terms and lovely things.

The ugly things we had to do
for the rest of our lives.

Opening the Will

I'm still in the room. Two days from now
I will see it from the outside only,
the closed shutter of your room where we loved one
  another
and not all mankind.

And we shall turn to the new life
in the special way of careful preparations
for death, turning to the wall
as in the Bible.

The god above the air we breathe
the god who made us two eyes and two legs
made us two souls too.

And we shall open these days
on a day far away from here, as one opens
the will
years after a death.

My Mother

My Mother Died on Shavuot

My mother died on Shavuot when they finished
    counting the Omer,
her oldest brother died in 1916, fallen in the war,
I almost fell in 1948,
and my mother died in 1983.
Everyone dies at some counting,
long or short,
everyone falls in a war,
they all deserve a wreath and a ceremony and an
    official letter.
When I stand at my mother's grave
it's like saluting
and the hard words of the Kaddish a salvo
into the summer skies.

We buried her in Sanhedria next to my father's grave,
we kept the place for her
as in a bus or cinema:
leaving flowers and stones so no one would take her
    place.

(Twenty years ago this graveyard was
on the border, facing the enemy's positions.
The tombstones were a good defense against tanks.)

But in my childhood there was a botanical garden here
lots of flowers with frail wooden tags
bearing names of flowers in Hebrew and Latin
Common Rose, Mediterranean Sage,
Common Scream, Tufted Weeping,
Annual Weeping, Perennial Mourning,
Red Forget-Me-Not, Fragrant Forget-Me-Not,
Forget-me-not, forget.

Now She Descends

Now she descends into the earth,
now she is on a level with the telephone cables,
    electrical wires,
pure water pipes and impure water pipes,
now she descends to deeper places,
deeper than deep where lie
the reasons for all this flowing,
now she is in the layers of stone and groundwater
where lie the motives of wars and the movers of
    history
and the future destinies of nations and peoples
yet unborn:
My mother, Satellite of Redemption,
turns the earth
into real heavens.

From Jerusalem to the Sea and Back

From Enclosed Jerusalem

I went from enclosed Jerusalem toward the open sea
as to the opening of a will. I went
on the old road. A bit before Ramla,
on the side of the road, still stand
tall, strange hangars,
half-ruined, from the World War:
there they checked engines of airplanes,
their noise silenced the whole world.
Pure flying was hoarded then
for all my life.

The Soul

I travel. Travels are the soul
of this world. Travels remain forever.
It's so simple: a green mountain slope growing trees
     and grass,
and on the other side, a dry mountain slope, charred
     by the hot wind,
I travel between them. Simple logic of the sunny side
and the rainy side. Blessing and curse, justice and
     injustice,
I travel between them. Wind of the sky and wind of
     the earth,

wind against me and wind with me. Hot love and cold
    love
like the migration of birds. Travel, my car.

Not Far from Death

In Latrun,* not far from the death on the hill
and the silence in the buildings, stands a woman
on the side of the road. Next to her, a shiny new car,
motor gaping as in amazement, waiting
to be towed to a safe place.
The woman is beautiful. Her face, confidence and rage.
Her dress a love banner. A very passionate woman,
inside her stands her dead father
like a quiet soul. I knew him alive,
I greeted him when I passed by.

An Old Bus Stop

I passed an old bus stop where I stood
many years ago, waiting for a vehicle to take me
to someplace else.

There I stood, consoled before loss
and healed before pain, resurrected
before death and full of love before separation.

---

*Latrun is both a Trappist monastery and the site of a fierce battle in the
Israeli War of Independence.

There I stood. The groggy fragrance
of orange groves in blossom anesthetized me
for all the years to come, to this very day.

The stop is still there. God is still
called "Place," and I, sometimes,
call Him "Time."

Sunflower Fields

Fields of sunflowers ripe and withering,
brown and wise, need the sun no more but sweet
shadow, internalized death, the inside of a drawer,
a sack deep as the sky, their World-to-Come,
dark of a house, the inside of a man.

I at the Sea

I at the sea. Sailboats of many colors move
over the water. Next to them, I am a clumsy oil tanker
with a small white poop deck,
my body is heavy and my head small, thinking
or not thinking. Did think.

In the sand I saw a girl learning to dress
or undress in public under a huge towel:
what a wonderful dance of her body. What a hidden
    serpent movement,

what a struggle between dressing and undressing,
between Jacob and his angel, between lover and
    beloved.

The towel drops from her body as from a statue
    unveiled.
The girl won. She laughs. She waits.
And perhaps they wait for her in a tearful place.
She is more beautiful than me, and younger.
I am more prophet than her.

And I Return

And I return to Jerusalem. I sit on my seat
but my soul stands inside me like a congregation
    praying:
Holy, Holy, Holy. Travel, my car.
On a small hill beside the road tanks were standing,
no more. Now carob trees at dusk,
a male carob and a female carob from another world
    that is pure love.
The tremor of their leaves in the wind is like the
    tremor of precision instruments
measuring the unmeasurable.
And the shadows that will merge and will be called
    night,
and we who will be called by our full names
by which we are called only in death.

The night of never-again will come again.
I return to my home in Jerusalem and our names will
   be lost
among these hills like shouts from the mouths of
   searchers.

Four Resurrections in the Valley
of the Ghosts

First Resurrection

A woman who looks like my mother sees a man who
   looks like me,
they pass each other without turning around.

Mistakes are marvelous and simple as life and death,
as the arithmetic book of a small child.

In the shelter for wayward girls, girls singing on the
   balcony
hang their clothes out to dry, banners of love.

In the fiber institute they make ropes of fiber
to bind souls in the bundle of life.

An afternoon wind blows, as if asking:
what did you do, what did you talk about?

In old stone houses young women do in the day
what the mothers of their mothers dreamed of doing at
   night.

The Armenian Church is empty and closed
like an abandoned wife whose husband went far off
  and disappeared.

Wayward girls sing, "God will bring the dead to life
in His great mercy," and fold their dried clothes.
"Blessed forever be His name."

Second Resurrection

In the public park, pots that once held plants—
now empty and crumpled like discarded wombs.

Seesaws and slides, like instruments of torture
or like wings of a big bird or a falling angel.

And the ancient ceremony begins,
a father tells his little son:

"So I'm going,
and you stay here alone."

So are summer and winter in their due time, so are
generations in their changes, so those who remain,
  those who go.

Third Resurrection

With the pleading voice of a beggar,
I praise the world.

With a voice crying for help from the depths,
I laud.

A young woman curses her mother
who left her fat thighs.

I bless her
and her too.

Sadness of lovers parted
is empty here, hollow as a drum.

People wrote on the gate of their home:
"Strangers No Entrance"
but they themselves are strangers.

At the wall of the Christian cemetery
a violated telephone booth,
the torn wires hanging, like veins
and arteries: waiting for their time.

Fourth Resurrection

I saw the seats of a torn-down movie house
lying in an empty lot,
taken out of their dark home
and abandoned to the cruel sun,
broken seats with fragments of numbered rows:
24, 26, 28, 30 with 7, 9, 11, 13.

And I asked myself: Where are the feats and where are
    the words
that were on the screen. *Who in fire and who in water,*
and where are those who sat in these seats,
where is their lament and where is their laughter,
where are their roads and where are their oaths,
and what are the sights and the images they see,
and what are the words they hear now?
Are they still sitting in numbered rows
or standing in long lines,
and how will they arise to life and where.

I Am a Poor Prophet

I am a poor prophet. Like a poor boy with only
two colors: I paint my life in war
and in love, in clamor and in silence.

The great prophets threw out half their prophecies
like the half-smoked cigarette butts of a nervous
    smoker.
I pick them up and roll myself some poor prophecies.

In full water towers the water is silent,
in empty pipes, the no-water gurgles and snores.

Words soak up "blood, sweat, and tears"
and are thrown out in the ashcan. Disposable words,
like Kleenex. Disposable people,
this is their eternity.

Words should have been empty
and narrow and tough, like a watershed.
Despair and hope, joy and sorrow, calm and rage
should have flowed in two sides,
in a new cycle.

I am a poor prophet. I live inside the hope of others
as inside a beam of light not meant to shine on me.

I cast a shadow in my own image, like my own figure.
I hide in me a famous and beautiful view,
my body comes between the seer and the sight.

I am a prophet with no profit who comes back home
   at lunchtime
to eat and rest and at night to sleep.
I have an annual vacation, a sabbatical,
Soul Security and a retirement pension.

I started my life so low.
When I climb high with my intoxicated soul,
when I reach the peak of my visions,
I find myself with everyday people
who have children and work, family cares,
household chores. These are my visions.
I am a poor prophet.

Summer Evening at the Window
with Psalms

Careful examination of the past.
Why is my soul disquieted within me like the souls
in the nineteenth century before the great wars,
like curtains that want to free themselves
from the open window and fly away.

We console ourselves with short breaths
like after running. We heal ourselves
always. We want to reach death
hale and healthy, like a murderer
condemned to death, wounded when he was caught,
whom the judges want to recover before the gallows.

I think: how many *still waters*
can give one still night,
and how many *green pastures,* wide as the desert,
will give one hour of peace,
and how many *valleys of the shadow of death* do we need
to cast a shadow full of compassion in the cruel sun?

I look through the window: one hundred and fifty
psalms pass through the twilight,

one hundred and fifty psalms, big and small,
what a great, splendid, passing fleet!

I say: the window is God
and the door is His prophet.

Summer Rest and Words

The sprinklers calm summer's wrath.
I am content with the sound of the sprinkler going
    round
and the swish of the water on leaves and grass.
My wrath spent and calm and my melancholy full and
    quiet.
The newspaper drops from my hand and turns back
    into
passing time and paper wings,
then I shut my eyes,
and return to the words of the rabbi in my childhood
on the bima of the synagogue: "And give eternal
    salvation
to those who go off to their world." He changed
the words of the prayer a little, he did not
sing and did not trill and did not sob
and did not flatter his God like a cantor
but said his words to God with quiet confidence,
    demanded,
in a calm voice that accompanied me all my life.

I ask myself what did he mean by these words,
is there salvation only for those who go to their rest?
And what about our world and what about mine?
Is rest salvation or is there any other?

And why did he add eternity to salvation?
Words accompany me. Words accompany my life
like a melody. Words accompany my life
like the words at the bottom of a movie screen,
    subtitles
translating their language into mine.

I remember, in my youth translation sometimes
lagged behind the words, or anticipated them,
the face on the screen was sad, even crying,
and the words below were joyful, or things lit up
and laughed and the words spelled great sadness.
Words accompany my life.
But the words I say myself
are now like stones I fling
into a well in the field, to test
if it is full or empty,
and its depth.

Autumn Is Near and Memory
of My Parents

Autumn is near. The last fruit ripens.
People walk on roads they never walked on.
The old house begins to forgive its tenants.
Trees darken with age and people whiten.
Rain will come. The smell of rust will be fresh
and pleasant like the smell of blossoming in the spring.

In the northern countries they say most leaves
are still on the trees, and here we say
most words are still on the people,
our foliage loses other things.

Autumn is near. Time to remember my parents.
I remember them like the simple
toys of my childhood
revolving in little circles,
humming quietly, raising a leg,
lifting an arm, turning a head
from side to side, rhythmically, slowly,
a spring in their belly and the key in their back.

Suddenly, freezing, they remain
forever in their last gesture.

That is how I remember my parents.
And how they were.

Little Ruth

Sometimes I remember you, little Ruth,
we were separated in our distant childhood and they
    burned you in the camps.
If you were alive now, you would be a woman of
    sixty-five,
a woman on the verge of old age. At twenty you were
    burned
and I don't know what happened to you in your short
    life
since we separated. What did you achieve, what
    insignia
did they put on your shoulders, your sleeves, your
brave soul, what shining stars
did they pin on you, what decorations for valor, what
medals for love hung around your neck,
what peace upon you, *peace unto you.*
And what happened to the unused years of your life?
Are they still packed away in pretty bundles,
were they added to my life? Did you turn me
into your bank of love like the banks in Switzerland
where assets are preserved even after their owners are
    dead?
Will I leave all this to my children
whom you never saw?

You gave your life to me, like a wine dealer
who remains sober himself.
You sober in death, lucid in the dark
for me, drunk on life, wallowing in my forgetfulness.

Now and then, I remember you in times
unbelievable. And in places not made for memory
but for the transient, the passing that does not remain.
Like in an airport, when the arriving travelers
stand tired at the revolving conveyor belt
that brings their suitcases and packages,
and they identify theirs with cries of joy
as at a resurrection and go out into their lives;
and there is one suitcase that returns and disappears
    again
and returns again, ever so slowly, in the empty hall,
again and again it passes.
This is how your quiet figure passes by me,
this is how I remember you until
the conveyor belt stands still. *And they stood still. Amen.*

Sheepskin Coat

My good friend gave me a sheepskin coat
on a cold winter day in a distant land.
The coat turned me into an inside-out sheep,
the woolly fur inside and the skin outside,
I am an internalized sheep maaing inside.
I don't know if the coat will keep off rain and snow
or will absorb them and make me heavy,
but it will protect my internal world.
My internal world perhaps is no more
than a collection of rags and junk
the crazy collector gathered to soothe himself.
And maybe I do not live inside my life,
like a streetlamp, its light living
in a dark room while it stands outside.

The coat is brown on the outside and white inside.
My eyes are earth-colored, my shirt has the color of a
    green field,
but fields do not give me bread, stores do.
And the twilight wind does not move stalks in the
    field
but buyers in shining halls
and people no longer for human use
but only for vain ornament—like horses

or like candles, once used for light
and now only for a passing holiday or a fleeting
   memory.
Everything changes. Everything changes,
sleep shivers from cold and chaos,
memories explode and sink like ashes,
continuity bursts like a thin paper bag,
every passing car tears off of me
a layer of life, dreams are hard as ice
and cold as ice and melt like ice and are forgotten like
   water.
Times change places and landscapes move to another
   place
but I remain like a telephone pole
without wires above,
I am faithful as a water pipe,
even when the water streams in other channels.

My friend gave me a sheepskin coat made
in a distant place in the Andes Mountains:
gave me warmth from overseas, indulgence from afar.
I did not see the sheep alive or their shepherds,
I did not see the meadow or the hands
that stroked this sheep or the hands
that slaughtered it and skinned it
or the mouths that ate its meat
and sang songs of high mountains after they ate their
   fill.

The sheepskin coat is alien among the sheep of our
    land
who slide down the Hermon and graze in the
    Mountains of Ephraim.
But it will get used to it as people do,
like the eucalyptus trees who brought their aroma
    from afar,
without forgetting, without getting tough,
like the soft Bible in a hard binding
I still want to kiss with my lips
when it falls from the table to the floor.

Man with Knapsack

Man with knapsack in the marketplace, Brother,
like you, I am a donkey man, a camel man,
an angel man, I am like you.
Our arms are free like wings.
Compared to us, all who carry full baskets
are slaves of slaves bound and pulled down.

We exchange coins for fresh vegetables,
and for the forgetting of our lives we buy
fruit and their memories, memory of field and garden,
memory of the smell of earth and the buzzing of bees
  on a hot day.

We saw a woman in a light summer dress
before a great and heavy love
which will determine her life. She doesn't know yet
but we do. On our back
we carry fruit from the tree of knowledge.

Man with knapsack, where do you live?
I am like you, we live in the distances
between reward and punishment.
And how do you live? And how do you sleep at night,
what do you dream of? People you love,
do they still live in the same places?

Our knapsacks like folded parachutes
on our backs, at night they open wide
so we can jump, hovering
into the fragrance of remembering and forgetting.

My Son

Because of love and because of making love
and because the pain of the unborn
is greater than the pain of the born,
I said to the woman: "Let us make a man
in our own image." And we did. But he grows
different from us,
day by day.

Furtively he eavesdrops on his parents' talk,
he doesn't understand but he grows on those words
as a plant grows without understanding
oxygen, nitrogen, and other elements.

Later on he stands before the opened
holy arks of legend
and before the lighted display windows
of history, the Maccabean wars, David and Goliath,
the suicides of Masada, the ghetto uprising,
Hannah and her seven sons,
he stands with gaping eyes
and, deep down, he grows a vow like a big flower:
To live, to live, not to die like them.

When he writes, he starts the letters from the bottom.
When he draws two fighting knights

he starts with the swords, then come the hands,
and then the head. And outside the page
and beyond the table—hope and peace.

Once he did something bad in school
and was punished: I saw him,
alone in an empty classroom,
eating with the gestures of a tamed beast.
I told him, fight me
but he fights the school,
law and order.
I told him, pour out your wrath on me
but he caresses me and I caress him.

The first real
big school outing
is the outing from which
they never return.

Hymn to a Masseuse

You are the *rose of Sharon, the lily of the valleys*
and I an aging male animal full of memories
about the Sharon and the valleys and lots of lilies.

I gave my back to the smiters, my tears
I turned into perfume, my sweat into spice
and my sighs into a soothing melody,
the cycle of my blood wells up in me
like the cycle of prayers on holidays.

You knead me as your hands please,
strong hands *like the hands of Esau from the field*
and sweet like *the voice of Jacob.*
The traces of clothes on my skin are erased
like the traces of tefillin from my childhood, like traces
of hard straps from my wars,
like traces of this world
that will be erased in the world to come.

You turned my body into my soul,
the soles of my feet into a face
(and they sing hallelujah).
The triple brain between my legs is light and
   thoughtless,

the ass is the messiah full of salvation,
an all-forgetting messiah.

My mouth sucks on the cracks of closed windows
and on keyholes of locked doors,
my mouth sucks and I fill up like a baby,
like a sated bedbug landed on his back.
Silly baby sucking everywhere,
"Silly baby! Suck, don't bite,
you're hurting, you're spoiling it all."

You left and I was left lying
like chairs in a restaurant at night overturned
on a table, legs spread and hands up
as in a prayer, a vain prayer.

With no yesterday no tomorrow
no beginning and no end
like God
without God.

The Greatest Desire of All

Instead of singing hallelujah, a curtain waves in an
  open window.
Instead of saying amen, a door closes, a shutter is shut.
Instead of the vision of the end of days
the voice of banners flapping in an empty street after a
  holiday.

Reflections take over the house,
float in the mirror, in the goblet.

I saw slivers of glass gleaming in the sun
in the Judean Desert, celebrating a wedding
with no groom, no bride, pure celebration.

I saw a big and beautiful parade passing in the street,
I saw policemen standing between the spectators and
  the procession,
their faces to the viewers,
their backs to all that passed with trumpets and joy
  and banners.
Perhaps to live like this.

But the greatest desire of all is to be
in the dream of another,
to feel a slight pull, like reins,
to feel a heavy pull, like chains.

Deir Ayub, a Heap of Watermelons and the Rest of My Life

Deir Ayub, a heap of watermelons and the rest of my
   life.
An attack of sweetness in the room. I hear
the sound of passing cars outside and the sound of an
   airplane in the sky
like a dialogue at a nearby table and suddenly
an erection. The words from both sides of the equation
part from one another. Only the equal sign remains
like a buckle, for the release from a vow, an oath,
for the release of a buckle in love. Attack of sweetness
   in the room.

Deir Ayub at the entrance to the valley,
heap of watermelons next to the wall
and the rest of my life here. I hear the children of my
   childhood
sing songs for the memory of the dead, *"Therefore
my heart is glad and my glory rejoiceth but my flesh
shall rest in hope,"* and suddenly—erection
like the erection when you wake from a dream
which remains, even when the dream is forgotten.

Changes, Mistakes, Loves

In the summer, in a big park among the trees, I saw
a young man and a young woman photographing one
    another
on the lawn sloping down. Then they changed places
and whoever comes in his place and in her place,
    will be
like the difference between a cypress and a pine.

Oh changes, oh mistakes,
most loves are a mistake like the mistake of Columbus
who came to America and thought he had reached
    India,
and called the continent India,
so lovers say love,
the land of my love, my love.

Oh dark snooker game,
billiard balls clacking, falling into depths,
and the loneliness of he who remains alone at the
    table.

Oh tennis games in black garb
and nets eternally dividing.

In a very distant land, I once heard a girl
playing on a violin "Eli, eli,
she-lo yigamer le-olam"* so sweetly.

On a violin, with no words, far from the death
of Hannah Senesh and far from the white shore.
The same song, perhaps a lovesong to God,
perhaps to man, perhaps to the sea, perhaps
Caesarea, perhaps Hungary,
perhaps death, perhaps life.

*"My God, my God, let it never end." From a song by Hannah Senesh, a
native of Hungary and member of Kibbutz Sdot Yam (Caesarea), who
parachuted into occupied Hungary and was executed by the Nazis.

The First Rain on a Burned Car

Life close to death
at the body of a car on the roadside.

You hear the drops of rain on rusty tin
before you feel them on the skin of your face.

Rain came, salvation after death.
Rust more eternal than blood, more beautiful than the
    color of flames.

Shock absorbers calmer than the dead
who will not calm down for a long time.

Wind that is time alternates
with wind that is place, and God
remains on earth like a man who thinks
he forgot something and stays
until he remembers.

And at night you can hear,
like a wonderful melody, man and machine
on their slow road from a red fire
to black peace and from there to history
and from there to archaeology and from there

to the beautiful strata of geology,
this too is eternity and great happiness.

Like human sacrifice that turned into animal
sacrifice and then into prayer with a loud voice,
and then into prayer in the heart
and then without prayer.

Ramatayim

People sit on the porch
like ancient heroes at their tent door
recovering from imaginary wounds.

Their voices hanging on the banister
like clothes drying, pants and undershirts,
shirts and underpants, thigh's moaning and knee's
    crying,
song of legs and womb, screams of neck and armpit,
the cut off laughter of a breast.

From the wall, faucets stand out like prophets,
some running, some off.

Bread and circuses go on all summer,
statistics and eternal pain,
summer accounts and planning for the end,
the end of the day and the end of all days.
On the wall a painting of the sunset
in a snowy northern land, the sun itself
sets beyond the last orange grove.
(A girl's scent like the scent of citrus blossoms.)

The watch souls begin to bark,
the sweet cake wounded to death,
the sugar fell in the war.

Deganya

Water from last night in the puddles,
seeds from last season in the earth,
the earth from thousands of years ago.

All the things that happened before I was born,
at a time when they called the newborn
by the name of what happened when he was born
and the hills by the name of a beautiful god
and the springs by the name of love or death.

Reeds grow at the water
but also at the memory of water.
In the sky God's hammocks.
And among the palms and eucalyptus trees—
what's left for a man
but to surrender himself in happiness,
to donate his blood and his kidneys,
to donate his heart and his soul to others,
to belong to another, to be another.

In the old graveyard, buried together,
one dead of cholera and a baby that died at birth
and Eve, daughter of Erich Falk, who died
at eighteen years of age, far from her father's home.

And all the things that happened before I was born
meet the things that will happen after my death
and close me all around
and leave me behind
far away, forgotten and calm.

And what was sown by mistake of a wind was
   absorbed in the earth,
and what was flown by the caprice of a bee lives on,
and what was spread unwittingly by a passing shoe
goes on growing by its laws and its cycles,
and what laughed by mistake goes on laughing,
and what cried weeps in the rain,
and what died by error
goes on resting in death.

Hadera

"I never was in Hadera" is like
a verdict killing by sorrow and establishing a fact, like
   death.
"I just passed through and didn't stay."

The Street of the Heroes I understand,
I understand heroes and their death.
The water tower I understand,
but I never stayed in Hadera.

The roads of my life I thought were roads
were only light bridges
above places where I never was.

In the old houses the tiles still perform
the tapping of a dance that was.
Hosts forgot whom they invited
guests didn't know they were invited
and didn't come and those who could have met didn't
   meet.

People had hopes like eucalyptuses,
they were brought from far away and remained.
And in the abandoned orchard, citrus trees beg
for a fence around them as a soul

begs again for a body. The pumping shed is ruined,
an old engine rusting outside like an old man at the
   end of his days
sitting in the door of his house full of years,
at its side the remnants of a spring, throbbing weakly
in the scum of a shallow swamp, as a memory.

What determined my life and what didn't.
Oh summer 1942, oh Hadera
where I only passed by and didn't stay.
Had I stayed my life would be different.

Beit Guvrin

People scratched their names
on walls of the cave and went off or died,
thus their souls were created, names and souls.

Oh, my dead, my landscapes, my skies,
I am so heavy and aimless
like weights without a scale.

And once I was a scale without weights,
rising and falling easily, like a swing.

The voice of a turtledove laments even at his wedding
and the bees in their white hives
make real honey here in the dry hills
far from the blossom of the lush Sharon.

I saw children roaming and heard their merriment
passing from one cave to another.

Oh, holy despair of parents,
oh, sweet disappointment of teachers,
oh, their smell and oh, their spirit.

Words come to me now like flies
and like wasps, they are drawn to the wet in me

and the dry in me, to the sweet and to the bitter in
  me,
to the full and to the empty,
to the living and the dead and the rotting in me,
to the dark in me and to the light. Words forever.

Open Internalized

Open window. On the television screen colors
caper and tremble, like life flickering out,
shoes strewn over the floor,
clothes on the chair and no person.
On a stretched line underwear drying
from the flood of forty days and forty nights.
Open closet like a face you remember,
on the table flowers with long stalks
like the roads of life a man snipped
and put in a vase.

Here too the question arises, where did they go,
where does all this lead?

In the restaurant on the sidewalk opposite, a woman
  sits
at a table, her gaze raised above her plate,
she connects with a distant satellite in space.
Prepares to take off.

Surplus of Flowers in the World

Surplus of flowers in the world
like the surplus of the coffee crop in Brazil
thrown into the sea. Surplus of flowers
adorns tables in empty rooms and tombstones.

The movement of trade in the world makes me
    peaceful
like the migration of birds. And a torn newspaper with
    a date
fluttering on the floor makes me feel light.

Fog enfolds the end of the year
and the beginning of the next. I am excused from
    knowing
what is in the future beyond the fog.

I am a useless watchman
of the holy nothing. I am happy.
I am like an artilleryman bereft of
his target and his enemies and his God
and his shells and his cannon.
He aims at emptiness, he aims
his face and his face is beaming.

Throw Pillows

Sometimes I still hear the world
and all that's in it, like a little boy who puts a watch
   to his ear
and hears the ticktock without understanding.

And in my childhood I had two old aunts
who had a sofa and on the sofa
they tickled me with long knitting needles and on the
   sofa
were throw pillows embroidered with
a swan and an angel and roses.

They embroidered and embroidered the world on the
   pillows
and embroidered me too on the darkness of their
   death.
They loved me. I was their messiah.
And they said: A child should not be undressed
or dressed by more than one person, because only
the dead are dressed by two or three after the
   cleansing.
And I was their messiah.

Yom Kippur

Yom Kippur without my father and without my
   mother
is not Yom Kippur.

From the blessing of their hands on my head
just the tremor has remained like the tremor of an
   engine
that didn't stop even after their death.

My mother died only five years ago,
she is still being processed
between the offices above and the papers below.

My father who died long ago is already resurrected
in other places but not in my place.

Yom Kippur without my father and without my
   mother
is not Yom Kippur.
Hence I eat to remember
and drink not to forget
and sort out the vows
and catalog the oaths by time and size.

In the day we shouted "Forgive us,"
and in the evening we cried "Open to us."

And I say forget about us, forget us, leave us alone
at the closing of the gate when the day is done.
The last ray of the sun refracted
in the colored glass window of the synagogue.
The ray of the sun is not splintered,
we are splintered,
the word "splintered" is splintered.

A Man's Soul

A man's soul is like
a train schedule
a precise and detailed schedule
of trains that will never run again.

Life

Like high mountain climbers who set up a base in the valley at the foot of the mountains and another camp and camp number two and camp number three at various heights on the road to the peak, and in every camp they leave food and provisions and equipment to make their last climb easier and to collect on their way back everything that might help them on their way down, so I leave my childhood and my youth and my adult years in various camps with a flag on every camp. I know I shall never return, but to get to the peak with no weight, light, light!

At the Seashore

Traces that met in the sand were erased.
Their owners too were erased in the wind of their
  unbeing.

The little became a lot and what was a lot will become
  infinite
as the sand on the seashore. I found an envelope,
an address on its front and an address on its back.
But inside, empty and silent. The letter
was read somewhere else, like a soul that left its body.

A happy tune that lingered at night in the big white
  house
now is full of longing and full of sand
like bathing suits hung on a line between two wooden
  poles.

Water birds scream when they see land
and people scream when they see calm.
Oh, my children, children of my head,
I made them with my whole body and my whole soul,
now they are the children of my head,
now I am alone on this shore
with sandweed, low and trembling.

This trembling is its language. This trembling is my
language.
We have a common language.

Museum at Akhziv

A big anchor stuck in the yard. It will wait for eternity
for the ship it lost. Its longing adorns the world,
its rust a banner for all that was lost and will not
    return.

And at the gate a heap of cannonballs
from centuries gone by. Balls that hit
and balls that missed. The collector did not distinguish.

From the roof, you see the western Galilee
flourishing and green, the fat of the land. The road
    cuts
through it deep, like the hems of a bathing suit tight
    on the flesh
of thighs and derrieres. Desired land.

And in the house, a jumble of things.
A threshing sledge from an ancient vision,
a pitchfork from the prophecies and mills
of dead people. Many tools to grind
and squeeze and crack and many tools to close and
    smooth,
tools to build and tools to destroy,
as in the Book of Ecclesiastes. But above all
handles whose tools were lost and only they remained.

What can we learn from this about the human soul
and all that was left? What can we learn
about the tools that were lost and the hands that held
them?

At dusk the sun goes down in the sea
like someone who heard about the death of a loved
one.

A man returns from the sea holding his shoes in his
hand
as if holding his soul in his hand.
A newspaper with a precise date flew away.
Two warships pass: one to the north and one to the
south.
Day-people change places with night-people.
I see the changing of the guard in the beam of a
flashlight.

On the mound over there, ancient graves open
at night. The opposite of flowers.

I Want to Confuse the Bible

An airplane passes over the fig tree
that is over *the man under his fig tree.*
The pilot is me and the man under the fig tree is me.
I want to confuse the Bible.
I want so much to confuse the Bible.

I believe in trees, not as they once believed,
my belief is truncated and short-lived—
till next spring, till next winter.
I believe in the coming of rain and in the coming of
   sun.
Order and justice are confused: good and evil
on the table before me like salt and pepper,
the shakers so alike. I want so much
to confuse the Bible. The world
is filled with knowledge of good and evil, the world is
   filled
with learning: birds learn from the blowing wind,
airplanes learn from the birds,
and people learn from all of them and forget.
The earth is not sad because the dead are buried in it.
As the dress of my beloved is not happy
that she lives in it.
the sons of man are clouds
and Ararat is a deep valley.

And I don't want to return home
because all bad tidings come home
as in the Book of Job.

Abel killed Cain and Moses entered
the Promised Land and the Children of Israel stayed in
   the desert.
I travel in Ezekiel's divine chariot
and Ezekiel himself dances like Miriam
in the Valley of Dry Bones.
Sodom and Gomorrah are booming towns
and Lot's wife became a pillar of sugar and honey
and *David King of Israel is alive.*
I want so much
to confuse the Bible.

My Children

I don't know if I shall have a share in the
   World-to-Come,
but in the world of my children, I will have no share.

I am not a prophet and not the son of a prophet
but I am a father of prophets. My children
light up the next century like spotlights.

Their games will be realized like prophecy
and their toys will come to life.
They are noise and silence and noise,
they are sea and land and air,
they are the skies and all their hosts.

Their longing for their future
and my longing for my childhood
pass by one another without meeting
like the fatal error of a tunnel engineer.

My daughter has little red shoes,
my two sons wear shoes my size,
but they don't have my father
and they don't have his God,
they have only me like a toy bear, big and hairy,
to stroke and play with,

so they will remember me and mention me to their
  children.
And they will remember that Ben Gurion was an
  airport
in the days when there still were airports
that remember the man and the rest of the deeds he
  did.

And I, sometimes, call the highway "King's Road,"
though *there is no king in Israel*
and everyone does what is right in his own eyes.

The Jews

The Jews are like photos in a display window,
all of them together, short and tall, alive and dead,
brides and grooms, bar mitzvah boys and babies.
Some are restored from old yellowed photographs.
Sometimes people come and break the window
and burn the pictures. And then they start
photographing and developing all over again
and displaying them again, sad and smiling.

Rembrandt painted them wearing Turkish
turbans with beautiful burnished gold.
Chagall painted them hovering in the air,
and I paint them like my father and my mother.
The Jews are an eternal forest preserve
where the trees stand dense, and even the dead
cannot lie down. They stand upright, leaning on the
    living,
and you cannot tell them apart. Just that fire
burns the dead faster.

And what about God? God lingered
like the scent of a beautiful woman who once
faced them in passing and they didn't see her face,
only her fragrance remained, kinds of perfumes,
blessed be the Creator of kinds of perfumes.

A Jewish man remembers the succah in his
   grandfather's home.
And the succah remembers for him
the wandering in the desert that remembers
the grace of youth and the Tablets of the Ten
   Commandments
and the gold of the Golden Calf and the thirst and the
   hunger
that remember Egypt.

And what about God? According to the settlement
of divorce from the Garden of Eden and from the
   Temple,
God sees his children only once
a year, on Yom Kippur.

The Jews are not a historical people
and not even an archaeological people, the Jews
are a geological people with rifts
and collapses and strata and fiery lava.
Their history must be measured
on a different scale.

The Jews are buffed by suffering and polished by
   torments
like pebbles on the seashore.
The Jews are distinguished only in their death
as pebbles among other stones:

when the mighty hand flings them,
they skip two times, or three,
on the surface of the water before they drown.

Some time ago, I met a beautiful woman
whose grandfather performed my circumcision
long before she was born. I told her,
you don't know me and I don't know you
but we are the Jewish people,
your dead grandfather and I the circumcised and you
    the beautiful granddaughter
with golden hair: we are the Jewish people.

And what about God? Once we sang
"There is no God like ours," now we sing "There is no
    God of ours"
but we sing. We still sing.

The Land Knows

The land knows where the clouds come from and
   whence the hot wind,
whence hatred and whence love.
But its inhabitants are confused, *their heart is in the East
And their body in the far West.* *
Like migratory birds who lost their summer and winter
lost the beginning and the end and they migrate
to the end of pain all their days.

The land can read and write,
its eyes are open. It would be better
if it were ignorant as the people of the land,
blind and groping
for its children without seeing them.

The Greater Land of Israel is like a fat and heavy
   woman
and the State of Israel like a young woman,
supple and thin waisted,
but in both of them

*Line from a famous Zionist poem by Yehuda Halevi (1075–1141).

Jerusalem is always the cunt of the land,
the unsated cunt,
the throbbing and screaming orgasm
which won't end until Messiah comes.

Temporary Poem of My Time

Hebrew writing and Arabic writing go from east to
    west,
Latin writing, from west to east,
languages are like cats:
you must not stroke their hair the wrong way.
The clouds come from the sea, the hamsin from the
    desert,
the trees bend in the wind
and stones fly from all four winds,
into all four winds. They throw stones,
throw this land, one at the other,
but the land always falls back to the land.
They throw the land, want to get rid of it,
its stones, its soil, but you can't get rid of it.

They throw stones, throw stones at me
in 1936, 1938, 1948, 1988,
Semites throw at Semites and anti-Semites at
    anti-Semites,
evil men throw and just men throw,
sinners throw and tempters throw,
geologists throw and theologists throw,
archaeologists throw and archhooligans throw,
kidneys throw stones and gallbladders throw,

head stones and forehead stones and the heart of a
  stone,
stones shaped like a screaming mouth
and stones fitting your eyes
like a pair of glasses,
the past throws stones at the future,
and all of them fall on the present.
Weeping stones and laughing gravel stones,
even God in the Bible threw stones,
even the Urim and Tumim were thrown
and got stuck in the breastplate of justice,
and Herod threw stones and what came out was a
  Temple.

Oh, the poem of stone sadness
oh, the poem thrown on the stones
oh, the poem of thrown stones.
Is there in this land
a stone that was never thrown
and never built and never overturned
and never uncovered and never discovered
and never screamed from a wall and never discarded
  by the builders
and never closed on top of a grave and never lay under
  lovers
and never turned into a cornerstone?

Please do not throw any more stones,
you are moving the land,
the holy, whole, open land,
you are moving it to the sea
and the sea doesn't want it
the sea says, not in me.
Please throw little stones,
throw snail fossils, throw gravel,
justice or injustice from the quarries of Migdal Tsedek,
throw soft stones, throw sweet clods,
throw limestone, throw clay,
throw sand of the seashore,
throw dust of the desert, throw rust,
throw soil, throw wind,
throw air, throw nothing
until your hands are weary
and the war is weary
and even peace will be weary and will be.

We Have Done Our Duty

We did our duty.
We went out with our children
to gather mushrooms in the forest
which we planted ourselves when we were children.

We learned the names of wildflowers
whose aroma was
like blood spilled in vain.
We laid a big love on small bodies,
we stood enlarged and shrunken in turn,
in the eyes of the holder of the binoculars,
divine and mad.

And in the war of the sons of light and the sons of
    darkness
we loved the good and soothing darkness
and hated the painful light.
We did our duty,
we loved our children
more than our homeland,
we dug all the wells into the earth
and now we dig into the space of the skies,
well after well, with no beginning, no end.

We did our duty,
the words "you shall remember" we changed to "we
   will forget"
as they change a bus schedule
when the direction of the route changes,
or as they change the plaques
of "Dew and Showers" and "He Who Brings Rain" in
   the synagogue
when the seasons change.

We did our duty,
we arranged our lives in flowerbeds and shadows
and straight paths, pleasant for walking,
like the garden of a mental hospital.

Our despair is domesticated and gives us peace,
only the hopes have remained,
wild hopes, their screams
shatter the night and rip up the day.

We did our duty.
We were like people entering a movie house,
passing by those coming out, red faced
or pale, crying quietly or laughing aloud,
and they enter without a second glance, without
turning back, into the light and the dark and the light.
We have done our duty.

This Is the Life of Promises

This is the life of promises. The Greek priest
knows, the rabbi knows, the child at night knows,
my mother knew and died, the
    dead-may-God-revive-them know,
the one in the fire and the one in the water,
the one at his end and the one not at his end know
and are waiting together in the earth. Death promises
revival, and life promises death. The false prophets
prophesy infinite happiness,
the true prophets promise a bad and bitter end,
but a bad and bitter end is at least a sign
of a good beginning and perhaps of a good and sweet
    middle.
For this is the life of promises,
not a life of security. And this is not the promised
    land
this is the land of promises.

The rosemary blooms in loving purple,
dark orchards will produce shining fruit,
the beekeeper of Kfar Yonah in the Sharon Valley
scatters his hives all over the country
even in the Negev Desert, to make honey without him,
and he goes round the country, checking from time to
    time.

A tire thrown into the wadi
rests among the thorns like a martyred saint,
and the thorns wait for the softening springtime,
for this is the land of promises,
for this is the land of vows and oaths,
their keeping and their breaking make its
geography, tear up its valleys
and split its rifts, raise its hills,
crush its craters so they won't find rest,
and make dry riverbeds and fill tributaries with water
to extinguish love and hate and to calm the sea.

And people in this land—some climb up
a high observation tower to see the places
they came from, and next to them people climb up to
    see
the places where they want to go,
and they speak to each other excitedly
with maps in their hands and point all around:
"We'll go there, yes, on that road" or "From there
we came, there we walked, there we stayed a day or
    two,
there we spent the night."
And some remain at the top of the tower
and won't come down. For this is the land of promises.
And hope and disappointment make holidays
and birth and death make celebrations,
and the land promises skies and the sky promises

God and God promises the land,
for this is the land of promises
and this is the city of promises
and David's tomb is not his tomb
and Rachel's tomb is not her tomb
and the vows are not vows and the oaths are not oaths
and everything is masks and everything is masked
  with something else.
And beautiful women need to cover
their holy places—
a flowery dress before love,
a striped dress after,
many laces as of a tent in the desert,
many straps as of a sail in the sea
(and there is no sea in Jerusalem), a loop for the night,
hooks and snaps for the day. The soul is a zipper,
the soul is buttons. A golden tiara on the brow,
a broad belt around the waist, and a shining buckle
is a crown of the lower kingdom
promising higher love, for this is the city
of promises.

In the narrow lanes near the Church of the Holy
  Sepulcher
I saw groups of Greeks, old men and women
straying confused, like an ancient Greek chorus
that lost its tragedy.
I saw them wearing black,

folded chairs gripped under their armpits
like folded wings.

And most of them will be dead a year from now,
like birds returning to their home from their home,
for this is the city of promises
and this is the land of promises
and this is the life of promises.